GW01072004

A LOAD OF NONSENSE!

ALTON DOUGLAS

Illustrations by Clive Hardy

To Alan
Here's to Nonsense!

Alton Douglas

BREWIN JUNIOR

First published by
Brewin Books Ltd, 56 Alcester Road,
Studley, Warwickshire B80 7LG in 2006
www.brewinbooks.com

ISBN 1 85858 400 0

A Cataloguing in Publication Record
for this title is available from the British Library.

Typeset in Futura
Printed in Great Britain by
Warwick Printing Company Limited.

CONTENTS

Ups And Downs	1
I'm The Bad Cowboy Spider, That's Me!	2
Eyes Left	4
Feet First	4
Protection Guaranteed	5
Inside Job	6
What Grows Up?	7
Fly Past	7
A Python Has Swallowed Our Gladys	8
The Song Of The Puny Sheep Shearer	10
Bad Mood Day	11
Kuehneosaurus	12
Merry Autumn	12
That Hurts!	13
Yakkity Yak	14
The Dunnock	14
It's Got Whiskers On It	14
The Hang-Gliding Excursion	16
Anti-Anglers	18
Bumpy Crossing	20
Three Yawns For The Axolotl	20
The Nothing-Right Monster	21
How Volga!	22
Spring Is Here	24
The End	26
Pterry	27
Silent Hoarder	28
Nothing	30
Fit The Bill	30
A Jungle Saga	31
It's All Latin	32

Dave The Dragon	33
Grass Roots	34
Game Set	35
Cheers! Whoopee!	36
On The Web	36
Chew True	36
Crocodile Fears	37
Whoa, Noah	38
The Ellyworthy Knit	39
The Parrot Dinosaur	47
Paper Talk	48
Twinned With ----?	49
Host Ghost	49
Aunty Dot's Simple Plot	50
Striped Charmers	51
Get Your Own	51
Smarty Plants	52
Catch Plenty, Too	53
About Face	54
Nicked Names	55
Best Feet Forward	56
Now You See It...	56
Sharp Stuff	57
Snakes Alive	58
Spare A Thought	59
Trombone Blues	60
Buried Pleasure	61
The Sloth	62
Ready - Steady - Stop!	62
The Dodo	63
I'm Shy Of Sultanas	64
The Big Stiff	65

A LOAD OF NONSENSE!

A LOAD OF NONSENSE!

UPS AND DOWNS

As Denis the Diver was thinking
Of things such as eating and drinking,
A call from the ship
Said, "Abandon your trip
And just come on up quick 'cos we're sinking".

I'M THE BAD COWBOY SPIDER, THAT'S ME!

I'm the Bad Cowboy Spider,
The curse of the West,
I'm wanted on posters,
"The West's Biggest Pest".
I'd rustle some cattle,
I'd steal every head
But, trying to think
Of the neighbours instead,
I don't even rustle
My paper in bed.
I'm the Bad Cowboy Spider,
That's me!

I'm the Bad Cowboy Spider
Who robs all the banks.
I ask for their cash
But I never say thanks.
As soon as they chase me
I run off and hide.
The truth is I've not even
Learned how to ride –
I've still got to work out
Which legs go which side.
I'm the Bad Cowboy Spider,
That's me!

EYES LEFT

I'm not sure what the monster can be
The room is too gloomy to see.
He unblinkingly spies
With his dozens of eyes
But I wish they'd stop staring at me.

FEET FIRST

My sister Sharon bites her nails,
But happily it never shows.
Neglecting thumbs and fingers, she
Just concentrates on toes.

PROTECTION GUARANTEED

The bat's a protected species,
So that's OK for bats.
But I want to know what species
Protects us all from bats?

INSIDE JOB

An ostrich laid the perfect egg,
Then crawled inside and sat about,
"I'll wait for someone else", she said,
"To come along and hatch me out".

WHAT GROWS UP?

If you're confused with "stalactite",
Mistaking it for "stalagmite",
The "stalac" is the one with "c",
While "stalag" settles for a "g".
Now "c" should represent the "ceiling"
"g" the "ground" (you get the feeling?);
"c" comes down from roof to floor -
Or is it up? I'm never sure!

FLY PAST

Children aren't supposed to fly,
So if you see me whizzing by,
Just wave and I'll wave back and we
Can rest assured it isn't me.

A PYTHON HAS SWALLOWED OUR GLADYS

BURP!

A python has swallowed our Gladys,
I wasn't around to protest
But the evidence points
To an absence of joints
And I've looked everywhere
But I can't find the rest.

A python has swallowed our Gladys,
One gulp, it consumed every scrap,
From the bridge of her nose
To the nails on her toes,
(And including the budgie
Asleep on her lap).

A python has swallowed our Gladys,
I know what I'm talking about,
It's as simple as that,
It's still wearing her hat
And a voice from within says,
"It's dark - let me out!"

A python has swallowed our Gladys,
I'm sure that that's quite understood,
But I ought to confess
How I feel - can you guess?
Well, the word for the way

That I'm feeling is, "GOOD!"

TWEET!

THE SONG OF THE PUNY SHEEP SHEARER

When shearing sheep,
Because I'm weak,
I have to use a pulley.
Without the aid
Of ropes and wheels
They'd end up just as woolly.

At night in bed
Inside my head,
I have a secret sheep-wish:
I wish they'd learn
To shear themselves
And save me feeling sheepish.

BAD MOOD DAY

My dog's a pest, but as a pet he
Is preferable to any yeti
But if I had an anaconda
I know of which I'd feel the fonder.

KUEHNEOSAURUS

A lizard lived here long before us,
The Somerset Kuehneosaurus.
It floated gently like a glider
Then preserved itself in local cider.

MERRY AUTUMN

Late Oct/early Nov should bring us
First of many carol singers.
(Another reason
I hate the season).

THAT HURTS!

Porcupines can't understand
Why other animals avoid them,
They wonder was it something said
That could have frightened or annoyed them?
They simply cannot figure out
The pain that comes from prickly spines,
Their egos and their prides are hurt
Each time a creature even whines
And yet I know that porcupines
Would squeal and shout
And stamp about
If someone turned them inside out!

YAKKITY YAK

To think that I shall never crack
The face of this Tibetan Yak.
It never even coughs or chokes,
Suppressing laughter at my jokes.
I might as well address the wall –
I wonder if it's heard them all?

THE DUNNOCK

The Dunnock's an aggressive bird
That's often seen and often heard.
The male is an impulsive cock
Who barges in – but he dunnock.

IT'S GOT WHISKERS ON IT

The old man's whiskers grew and grew
(He knew they should be sheared).
They grew so big he sold his house
And moved into his beard.

The neighbours came and poked around
To see if he was in
And when they'd cleared enough away
They saw a friendly grin.

The council called about the rent,
It almost seemed unfair.
For how much could they charge for just
A mound of ginger hair?

And so they let him live in peace
And said, "Enjoy your cave"
But as they waddled off to lunch –
The old man had a shave!

THE HANG-GLIDING EXCURSION

Some animals flew in two-by-twos,
The squirrels, gnus and kangaroos
And some of them plumped for gang-gliding
At the hang-gliding excursion.

The walruses and rhinoceri,
A bison and my! A tsetse fly!
A bad-tempered wolf (with fang) gliding
At the hang-gliding excursion.

Each of them had a party pack,
Or carried a stack strapped on their back,
Whilst one took a small meringue gliding
At the hang-gliding excursion.

The monkeys, baboons and chimpanzees,
Gorillas with fleas and then (to please),
A nervous orang-outang gliding
At the hang-gliding excursion.

They included the hippopotamus
And polar bear Gus – but caused a fuss
By stopping the elephang gliding
At the hang-gliding excursion.

ANTI-ANGLERS

I watch the anglers settle right back
And wish, oh wish, the fish would fight back.

I'd like to see them swallowed whole
By aggravated carp or sole,
By tuna, turbot, sprat and plaice,
By maladjusted trout and dace,
Or savaged by a fearsome chub
Intent on treating man as grub,
Or stand and cheer as hunters feel
Intimidated by an eel,
Applaud the cruel and vengeful cods
That batter them with hooks and rods,
Or maybe give awards for biting
To halibut or hake or whiting.

And yet when nothing's being caught
It's lovely, so perhaps I ought
To just enjoy the rural scene
Of men relaxing by a stream
And think in peaceful terms pictorial
Concerning matters piscatorial.

BUMPY CROSSING

A kangaroo went bouncing by,
A baby in its pouch
And all I heard the baby say
Was   "Ouch!"   & "Ouch!"

                    & "Ouch!"

THREE YAWNS FOR
THE AXOLOTL

The Medieval Salamander
Lived in fire and acted grander
But meet the modern Axolotl –
Each one'll bore you (and the lot'll).

(In case that last line sounded crass,
They bore as singles or en masse).

THE NOTHING–RIGHT MONSTER

Now Gerald, as a monster,
Considers he's a flop.
He roars and then apologises,
Offering to stop.
He softens up his scaly bits
With something from a cup,
Then takes out all his teeth
Before he gobbles people down.

HOW VOLGA!

I love that funny Russian dance
They do down on their haunches,
The one that can't be done with plastic kneecaps
Or with paunches.
They fold their arms across their chests
And crouch as if to check their corns,
Then wildly kick out both their legs
Like acrobatic leprechauns.

On second thoughts, if that's the way
They all react to local drinks,
I'll cancel plans for Volga hols
And stick to Skegness, Lincs.

A LOAD OF NONSENSE!

SPRING IS HERE

The King decided, rather late,
Ancestral Homes were out of date.
To modernise he must begin
To draw the younger children in.
Although it seemed the strangest thing
The answer seemed to be a SPRING.

He rang up those receptionists
Of firms who'd send out sample lists.
Then settled down each night to log
The contents of each catalogue.
By email, telephone and fax,
He ordered goods from shelves and racks
And back they came, return of post,
(Or two days later, at the most).
The manufacturers of springs
All christened him the King of Kings.

He fastened springs to every wall,
To ceilings, floors and round the hall;
The contents of each precious parcel
Combined to build a Bouncy Castle.

A LOAD OF NONSENSE!

THE END

Let's talk about
The Duck this week
And focus on the
Tail and beak.

It dines without
A plate or cup,
That's headfirst in
And bottoms up.
I'd call that habit
Indiscreet,
With rear-view parts
And up-turned feet.

I don't admire
That attitude,
To me it seems
Extremely rude.
I wish the Duck
Would hide its end,
Reversing such
A vulgar trend.

I can't believe
They're doomed to sink,
Re-trained in handling
Food and drink.
You'll never hear
Of ducks that drown
With heads held high
And bottoms down.

PTERRY

Old Pterry, the sly Pterodactyl,
You'd have thought he was just like a bat till,
All wrinkled and dry,
Scarcely able to fly,
Just to win some affection he'd act ill.

SILENT HOARDER

I've been a naughty, selfish monk
Accumulating all this junk:
Tellys from the internet,
Fully mechanised roulette,
Black-jack table, licensed bar,
Motor bikes, a racing car,
Railway engine, books galore,
Helicopter parts and more,
Furniture from here to there,
A full-size model of a bear,
Something with a lengthy trunk
And even a retired monk.
There's hardly room to kneel and pray,
I've never thrown a thing away.
Neglecting all my studies – well,
I've never even learned to spell
And so I sit here in my habit
And dread a visit from the Abbit.

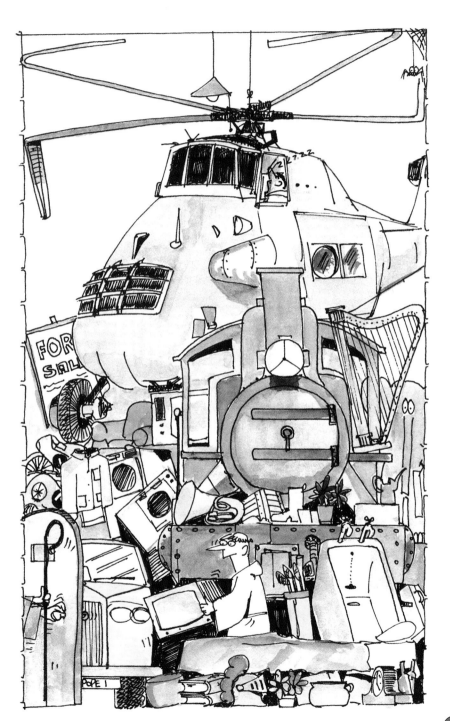

A LOAD OF NONSENSE!

NOTHING

We're covered all over with nothing
Surrounding our kneecaps and that.
It covers the lounge and the bedroom,
The kitchen, the loft and the cat.
It's in every garden and playground,
Each shop, every corner and wall.
It covers the whole of the country
And there's nothing like nothing at all.

FIT THE BILL

He'll never swallow
All of that
The greedy pelican.
You think he can't?
Just wait and see!
I know too welican.

SLURP!

A JUNGLE SAGA

Entangled in the undergrowth
He let out such a noise,
Followed by the sort of oath
That nobody employs,
A sordid mix of Arabic
And Bermondsey I'd say,
With just a dash of – take your pick –
And "Did he really say...?"
He biffed and boffed about a bit
And made the tangle worse,
Then made a bigger mess of it,
Repeating every curse.
His language caused a fly at last
To bite him low and deep,
The Tsetse said, "Perhaps, at last,
We'll all get off to sleep".

IT'S ALL LATIN

Maximus Cretinus
Oh, what a label!
Still he can't figure
His VII-times table.

DAVE THE DRAGON

DAVE THE DRAGON - BREATHING FIRE
AVAILABLE FOR DAILY HIRE,
FOR HEATING ROOMS OR STRIPPING PAINT
WITH GUARANTEE OF SELF-RESTRAINT

Until the day he lost control
And ate the local chippy whole.
A quick intake of breath occurred
And noises front and rear were heard,
As gas and flames conspired to heat
Poor Dave from head to scaly feet.
The gauge went up from warm to hot
And Dave exploded on the spot.

GRASS ROOTS

Eric noticed with the years
The hair just grew around his ears.
He sprinkled grass seed on his head,
"To see what happens", Eric said.

Now, where a sponge was once enough,
Electric mowers do their stuff.

GAME SET

From early days
I've always thought
Of tennis as
The oldest sport.
Remember how
The Bible taught
That Moses served
In Pharaoh's court?

CHEERS! WHOOPEE!

We're feeding our chickens
On whisky and corn,
Their fancies are really tickled:
They think that it's Christmas
The whole of the year
And their eggs are ready-pickled.

ON THE WEB

The crab to dig its seaside den
Must get each flo and ebb right.
I think I'll be a spider then
And build myself a web site.

CHEW TRUE

Year by year I've lost my teeth
(I've never really missed 'em).
One up, one down, that's all that's left
- my central eating system.

CROCODILE FEARS

The crocodile with baited breath,
(I'd baited it with Cousin Beth),
Broke off from a disgusting chew
And said, "I'll make a meal of YOU,
For if I gave you chance you'd choose
To make yourself a pair of shoes.
You'd clonk me with a club or sandbag
And with the remnants make a handbag".

WHOA, NOAH

As the warning of flooding was terribly stark
Noah was keen to deposit his ark.
Up on a hillside away from the damp
He watched as the animals mounted the ramp.

Then he noticed, with horror, the queue seemed to
    grow
And each of the creatures had someone in tow.
He cried, "It's outrageous to add to my troubles –
I've ordered singles and they've sent me doubles".

THE ELLYWORTHY KNIT

Mary Ellyworthy's hobby,
Which she'd learned from Uncle Bobby,
(Where he'd picked it up was anybody's guess),
Was a trifle antiquated
For a modern Miss and dated
Back to granny's far off childhood, more or less.

All her friends had fancy ringtones
But the thought would often bring tones
Of annoyance as she hated such excess.
With the others chasing pop stars
Little M awarded top stars
For the only thing she thought of as success.

She'd no time for any hero
(Even Beckham rated zero)
Or for film stars such as Law or even Pitt.
She disliked the latest crazes
Vulgar words and silly phrases
(Though she sometimes said,
"It's Cool" I must admit).

The age of laptops and computers
Left her cold and resolute as
All she wanted was to hide away and sit.
She'd no time for boys or fashion
For her solitary passion
Was to curl up with a ball of wool and KNIT.

A LOAD OF NONSENSE!

She'd start with something easy,
Knitting garments made her queasy,
(Almost no-ones knitted jacket ever fits).
She began with 'small and simple',
Cousin Jason's stylish pimple
And she even had a go at knitting nits.

She was fine with gloves and mittens
But her cats all turned out kittens
And her dolls and toys unravelled into bits
But, with patient application,
She received the school's ovation
With her mini Miss, the first of many hits.

But she still felt it was petty,
Nothing more than mere confetti,
Small in scale and insignificant as well.
For she longed to be amazing
To emerge with needles blazing
To create a *something* you could almost smell.

When her friends had made suggestions
Mary countered them with questions –
Were they silly? Does that really ring a bell?
A chimpanzee or a gorilla?
Or a bust of Charles' Camilla?
Or a gnome complete with fishing rod and well?

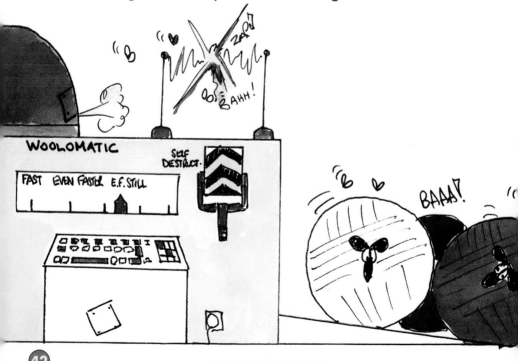

As for tying in with seasons,
She avoided for the reasons:
Far too obvious and quickly out of date.
Think of Santa when it's Summer?
And a Christmas bunny's dumber!
And an Autumn resolution's far too late!

No, it must be something splendid,
Show her needle power extended
Far beyond the reach of any sell-by-date.
Not a tiny jot or speck as
Nothing less than double deckers
Could have satisfied our Mary's present state.

She'd knit a model of the Station.
Then she heard a conversation,
Someone said that British Rail were leaving town.
She was bothered they'd announce all
Work must stop and that the Council
Would instruct some men to pull her model down.

So, she settled for a circus,
Its performers and its workers,
A marquee and, "Yes, I must include a clown.
Then some precious things and you'll be
Quite astounded at my jewellery
But has anyone a pattern for a crown?".

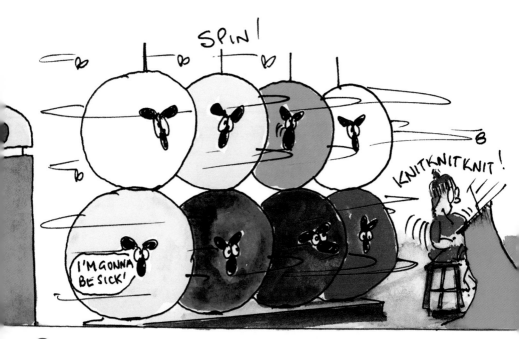

She knitted table loads of quiches,
Every size and every species,
(Then she found a friend from school
    had eaten one).
Herds of elephants and rhino
And that place – it's called – oh, I know!
It's the gardens hanging round in Babylon.

She wanted something for the climax
Say, a multi-duplex Imax,
Or the fan club that surrounded Elton John,
Or the Alps up to the fourth ridge,
Why, she'd even knit the Forth Bridge!
But the knitting might go on and on and on?

HAND - KNITTED

TILT!

She'd make a full-size Uncle Bobby!
Who'd inspired her choice of hobby,
(Though she'd often felt an urge to call him, "Sir").
So, she made a perfect likeness
(There were one or two she liked less)
But the final choice would please a connoisseur.

She was pleased with the improvement
But she failed to see a movement –
Uncle Bobby's woollen hands began to stir.
Then she looked – and was she dreaming?
Could it – Mary started screaming!
Uncle Bobby's clone had knitted one of HER!!!

THE PARROT DINOSAUR

That truly rare ornithopod,
The Parrot Dinosaur, was odd.
It imitated, like the bird,
Repeating everything it heard
And as a final act of folly
Went round roaring, "Pretty Polly!"

PAPER TALK

The finer points of Origami
Are just too much for ignorami.

(If English scholars show alarm I
Could make that last word "ignormai".)

TWINNED WITH ----?

When the face painters painted each other
A twin was the first with her mother
But they emptied the place
When the twin washed her face –
Underneath they discovered her brother.

HOST GHOST

I've never smelt sulphurous fumes
Or picked up sounds from empty rooms;
I don't believe in ghosts at all
And as for walking through a wall ------!

But when I look towards my feet
I have to say I'm incomplete,
Transparent parts of me I see
And wonder what became of me?

AUNTY DOT'S SIMPLE PLOT

Aunty Dot is such a snob,
She's advertised a gardener's job.
Which could be thought unorthodox –
She's only got a window box.

STRIPED CHARMERS

Beware the common antelope,
An arrogant, conceited dope,
That oversells its personal charm as
It lounges round in striped pyjamas.

GET YOUR OWN

They say that the hippopotamus
Can weigh as much as a London bus.
It's not that it's difficult to like
But I wouldn't let it near my bike.

SEE. NONE FOR AGES THEN THREE COME ALONG ALL AT ONCE.

SMARTY PLANTS

Talk to your plants,
Develop the knack –
I tried it today
But they answered
me back!

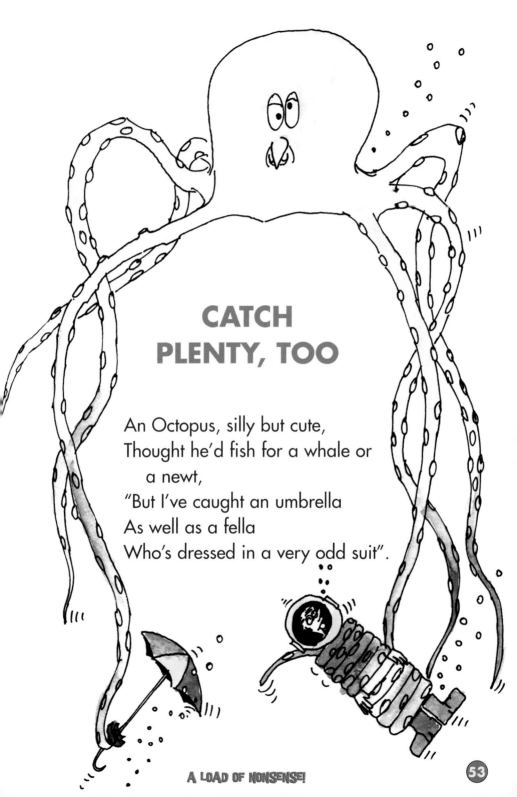

CATCH PLENTY, TOO

An Octopus, silly but cute,
Thought he'd fish for a whale or
    a newt,
"But I've caught an umbrella
As well as a fella
Who's dressed in a very odd suit".

ABOUT FACE

How dare you walk in backwards!
See the chaos that it brings?
The mind becomes accustomed
To the way of doing things.
And walking with your face
Behind your haircut isn't one
And poking bottoms round the door
Just simply isn't done.

I can't except you just forgot,
That's such a weak excuse.
You stand there with your back to me
And force me to deduce
It's down to bloody-mindedness,
The answer's in your past.
What else is there to think
About a nose that's always last?

I'm really such a simple soul,
Confusion mars my day.
Each time I look at you I find
You look the other way
And every conversation ends
Before it can begin,
For you look as if you're leaving
When you've only just come in.

NICKED NAMES

*Over the years I've collected quite a list of unusual
names. These are just some of them.*

Felicity Punter and Peregrine Gunter
And Hilary Willoughby-Smythe,
Philately Battersea, (even Roy Hattersley),
Gilda Matilda (nee Blythe),
Percy Pirantha and Charlie Chrysanthe-
Mum, Boris Zee, Morrisey James,
Henrietta Baretta, Loretta Coletta,
Are thinking of changing their names.

BEST FEET FORWARD

Concerning jobs, I've made a list
To try and find the busiest.
Do you know
Numero Uno?
A centipede's chiropodist!

NOW YOU SEE IT...

Oh, look! There's a little chameleon!
It's disguising itself on the wall
But it can't be a little chameleon
Or we wouldn't have seen it at all!

SHARP STUFF

A carpenter, know as Old Bissell,
Was threatened with instant dismissal
When he took to his bed,
With a pain in his head,
Caused by using his nose as a chisel.

SNAKES ALIVE

The sheep played a match with the cattle
(The football was more like a battle);
And a rattlesnake fan
Was the noisiest man
(There was no one else there with a rattle).

SPARE A THOUGHT

That busker's way of life's precarious
With a string and shoebox Stradivarius;

But compared with others it's a fine way,
(For example, try a home-made Steinway).

FRED'S PATENT PIANO TROLLEY

TROMBONE BLUES

*This ditty was inspired by my long-suffering friend,
John Clayton who, after watching my theatre act
from the wings, gave me the last two lines.*

I've not got the key to my trombone case,
I've just brought it out for the ride.
The last time I played it the man in the front
Lost his head on the end of my slide.

And I'm not gonna play in a marching band,
It's hard playing musical runs;
And I'm not gonna play in a circus band
'Cos I'm tired of them feeding me buns.

BURIED PLEASURE

Peking Man has played a hoax
By hiding all these years from folks;
But what about the "mammoth, large"?
They'd need a lot more camouflage.

Boo!

THE SLOTH

The sloth is such a boring clown
Enjoying hanging upside down
And when we pass it in the town
It's quite convinced WE'RE UPSIDE DOWN

READY - STEADY - STOP!

The tortoise and snail
Ran a two-handed race,
At a pace
They imagined was fast.
Their race was so slow,
That the record books show
Both of them
Finished up last!

THE DODO

The Dodo's name is always linked
With ancient birds they call "extinct".
If that's the case, as seems to me,
Who handles its publicity?

The Dodo gets a very good press,
Whilst others don't, I must confess.
Do you hear talk about the auk?
Do parrots rate a single squawk?
The spindly stork, the sparrow-hawk...
They seldom rate a line, or less.

The Dodo's fame continues on
And yet they claim it's dead and gone;
But if that happens to be true,
Then what's that sneaking up on you?

I'M SHY OF SULTANAS

This one came about because my young cousin came to tea one day, looked at a cake and said, "I'm shy of sultanas". She now works in a supermarket and is heartily embarrassed by the whole thing.

I'm shy of sultanas
And as for bananas
The red in my cheeks
Looks like paint.
At the mention of guavas
I'm terribly nuavas
And lychees have caused
Me to faint.

And then there's the orange,
Or anything forange,
I'm grapeful my paw-paws
Aren't seen,
For they shake like papayas -
But I'm not as shy as
My brother who's shy
Of a bean

A LOAD OF NONSENSE!

THE BIG STIFF

Arnold Palaver had just been accused
Of owning some muscles he'd not even used.
His wife had a job for him but he refused,
He said he was set in his ways.

So his wife went out shopping for Arnold instead,
For liquid cement, "To surprise him", she said,
Then lovingly tipped it all over his head.
Now he's certainly set in his ways.

For further copies of "A Load Of Nonsense!"
or Alton's other book of verses/cartoons,
"Shocking Nonsense!" or his biography,
"The Original Alton Douglas"
or any of his pictorial books on Birmingham,
Coventry, The Black Country, etc.
contact leading booksellers or for an ORDER FORM
please write to:

Alton Douglas
c/o Brewin Books Ltd,
Doric House, 56 Alcester Road,
Studley, Warwickshire B80 7LG, UK.

www.altondouglas.co.uk